Let's visit the
NETHERLANDS

RONALD SETH

BURKE

ACKNOWLEDGEMENTS

The author and publishers are grateful to the following individuals and organisations for permission to reproduce copyright photographs:

J. Allan Cash; Douglas Dickins; Keystone Press Agency Ltd., Max Koot and the Netherlands National Tourist Office.

The publishers are also grateful to Terry Mahon for assistance in the preparation of this edition.

The cover illustration is reproduced by permission of Spectrum Colour Library.

CIP data
Seth, Ronald
    Let's visit the Netherlands. – 2nd ed.
    1. Netherlands – Social life and customs – Juvenile literature
    I. Title
    949.2'073   DJ71
    ISBN 0 222 01018 5

Burke Publishing Company Limited,
Pegasus House, 116–120 Golden Lane, London EC1Y 0TL, England.
Burke Publishing (Canada) Limited,
Toronto, Ontario, Canada.
Burke Publishing Company Inc.,
Bridgeport, Connecticut, U.S.A.
Filmset in "Monophoto" Baskerville by Green Gates Studios Ltd., Hull, England.
Printed in Singapore by Tien Wah Press (Pte) Ltd.

Contents

The Land of Water

The Netherlands are sometimes known as Holland, and the people who live there are called the Dutch.

At first sight, the title of this chapter may not seem to make sense. How can you have a land of water? But it is not quite the nonsense it may appear to be, when you consider the Netherlands.

"Netherlands" means "low country". Precisely why it is so called is not known, some people having one explanation, others another, but one very good reason could be that at least two-fifths of it lie below sea-level.

A passenger steamer making its way along a broad stretch of the River Rhine as it flows through Holland to enter the sea at the Hook

If you look at the map you will see that the coast-line of the Netherlands has a number of deep inlets. They are not the same as the fjords of Norway, because the sea has cut out islands, especially where the great rivers, the Rhine and the Maas—which is known as the Meuse when it flows through France and Belgium—and several of their branches enter the sea at the Hook of Holland. There is also the great bay of the Zuyder Zee, sometimes called the IJsselmeer, and the nearby Waddenzee which is enclosed and shielded from the North Sea by a string of islands.

The land below sea-level is the land nearest to the coast. It exists only because a line of sand-dunes, higher than the sea, prevents the North Sea from flooding it. However, it would have been flooded long before now if the Dutch had not continually strengthened the dunes and replaced, by strong "walls", or embankments, known as dykes, those parts worn away by the sea.

Besides the deep inlets made into the coast-line by the sea, the Netherlands are crossed by the great rivers, the Rhine and the Maas, and a number of smaller ones. To prevent these rivers from inundating the countryside through which they flow (because their beds are constantly being raised by deposits of fresh earth and sand) they, too, have to be kept in their place by dykes.

Then, as well as the rivers, there are the canals. The whole country is criss-crossed by a vast network of man-made waterways, whose surfaces—and in many cases their beds—

The Zeeland Bridge—the longest bridge in Europe—part of the massive scheme to connect the former islands of the province and link them with the mainland

are often higher than the level of the country through which they flow. They, too, are prevented by dykes from flooding the countryside. These canals have three purposes: they are highroads for traffic, they act as drains, and they serve as boundaries for houses, fields and gardens—just as walls, hedges and ditches serve as boundaries in other countries.

Dutch canals are generally wide, usually just over thirty metres (about one hundred feet), with their depths varying from about two metres (six feet) to seven and a half metres (twenty-five feet). The greatest of all the Dutch canals, and, in fact, the widest and deepest in the world, is the North Sea Canal which joins the port of Amsterdam with the North Sea.

9

It is twenty-five kilometres (fifteen and a half miles) long, 122 metres (400 feet) wide and fourteen metres (forty-five feet) deep. It reaches the sea at the fishing village of IJmuiden, after passing through a set of locks so vast that the *Queen Elizabeth II* could pass through with over forty-five metres (150 feet) to spare at each end.

Canals, rivers and inlets take up one-fifth of the area of the Netherlands. The land surface is 34,367 square kilometres (about 13,000 square miles), roughly twice the size of Yorkshire, or one-sixteenth the size of France. But half of this area was once covered by the sea, which means that three-fifths of the Netherlands were once water. So the title of this chapter is not quite the nonsense it seems.

The people of the Netherlands first had the idea of turning some of their water areas into land more than three hundred years ago, when they undertook the immense task of filling in a number of lakes in North Holland. To give you some idea of the size of the job they gave themselves, one of these lakes alone, the Beemster Lake, had an area of 181 square kilometres (seventy square miles).

Two hundred years later, another huge scheme for reclaiming land was carried out. This time the Haarlem Lake, which was more than twice the size of the Beemster Lake, was filled in. But it was in 1918 that the Dutch government began in earnest to win back land from the sea.

Between 1918 and 1924 a dyke was constructed joining the island of Wieringen with the mainland, two and a half kilo-

A view of Marken, a village recovered from the Zuyder Zee by the "polder" system

metres (one and a half miles) away. This was followed by the building of an immensely heavy dyke thirty-two kilometres (nearly twenty miles) long, during the years 1927 to 1933, between Wieringen and Friesland. This dyke turned the Zuyder Zee into a lake, and the Dutch then began to fill it in.

Land won back from the sea in this way is called a *polder*. While building the dykes the Dutch began constructing the *polders*. The first of four large *polders* with which the Zuyder Zee was to be reclaimed was completed in 1930. It was next to the island of Wieringen and in area was 388 square kilometres (slightly more than 150 square miles). When the Second World War broke out (in 1939), the north-east *polder*, next to the mainland of Friesland, Drenthe and Overijssel was dry. It

11

was more than twice the size of the first, and during the war it began to produce wheat.

After the war ended in 1945, work was restarted on winning back land from the sea; it is still going on today. In the Zuyder Zee, the third *polder* was pumped dry and two more are planned. It will be many years before they are completed but, when they are, more than 202,345 hectares (500,000 acres) will have been reclaimed from the sea.

Building a *polder* requires great engineering skill. In the region of the Zuyder Zee, as you go along the roads you can see the huts of the groups of men called *polderjongens*, who are specially trained in the work. They come from Sliedrecht, in the province of South Holland. Ever since the first polders were begun three hundred years ago, men of Sliedrecht have carried out this work. The chief of the government department known as the *Waterstaat* has described them as "the workers who cán handle the unwieldy dredging-machines with unerring skill . . . who can strangle wild streams . . . those heavy-handed, slow-speaking men in long boots, who have travelled all over the world to do their work in mud".

At the last census, there were 14,200,000 Dutchmen living in the Netherlands. They speak a language which is not unlike German when you hear it spoken, but which looks very different when you see it written down. Dutch is, in fact, an off-shoot of the same Saxon language from which much of the English language also comes.

The Dutch have as their neighbours the Danes in the north, the West Germans in the east, and the Belgians in the south. The people living in the north of Belgium also speak Dutch, though they call the language Flemish.

The Netherlands are divided into eleven provinces, each of which has its own *Diet*, or parliament, which is responsible for the affairs of the province. To run the country, however, there is a parliament called the States-General.

The States-General has two "houses", like the British parliament. The *Eerste Kamer*, (First Chamber) has seventy-five members who are elected for six years by the provincial parliaments. The *Tweede Kamer* (Second Chamber) has one hundred and fifty members, who are elected by Dutch men and women over the age of twenty-one.

Unfortunately, there are many political parties in the

The States-General, the Hague

Netherlands, and eleven of them have representatives in the *Tweede Kamer*. The major parties are the Catholic People's Party and the Labour Party. But, because there are so many smaller parties, these two never have a large enough majority to form a government on their own. They have to make alliances with some of the smaller parties, and this always leads to difficulties in forming a government.

For some hundreds of years, the country of the Netherlands was a republic. In 1815, however, the Dutch voted to have a king. They chose a prince of one of the great families which had always been among the leaders of the nation—the House of Orange-Nassau. The present queen is Queen Beatrix of Orange-Nassau. She succeeded her mother, Queen Juliana, when the latter abdicated in 1980. There have been four consecutive queens since the appointment of Queen Emma as Regent in 1890. But Queen Beatrix and her husband (Prince Claus of the Netherlands) have three sons—and no daughters—so the Netherlands will one day have a king again.

The Dutch queen, like Queen Elizabeth II of England, is a constitutional monarch who rules the country through her Prime Minister and government. But she is less of a figure-head than the British monarch, as she presides over the Council of State which advises on all parliamentary bills. The Dutch Royal Family are very democratic, however, and may often be seen riding their bicycles in the streets of Amsterdam and The Hague.

14

The Netherlands' Past

In the Middle Ages, the Netherlands consisted of a "few duchies, cities and counties", ruled over by Spain. The Dutch were among the first nations in Europe to turn from the Roman Catholic religion to the Protestant religion in the middle of the sixteenth century.

King Philip II of Spain, who married Queen Mary Tudor of England and who, in 1588, sent the Great Armada against Queen Elizabeth I, was one of the strongest enemies of Protestantism. In an attempt to make the Dutch turn back to Roman Catholicism, he demanded very severe taxes from them. When the Dutch protested, he took no notice of them and, little by little, they began to resist until they broke out into open rebellion.

Queen Beatrix, the modern representative of the House of Orange

Their leader in this rebellion was Prince William of Orange. William was the son of William the Rich, whose vast estates he inherited. He was also the heir of the Prince of Orange, who owned great estates as well.

Shortly before the trouble with Spain began, William had left his father's estates in Nassau, in Germany, to take charge of the estates in the Netherlands belonging to the family. Because he was well-educated, and very intelligent and industrious—which was rare for a wealthy young prince in those days—the Dutch nobles accepted him as their leader.

When people quarrel about religion, they are apt to lose their tempers more fiercely than they do over any other kind of argument. There were many lost tempers in the Netherlands at this time, and many arguments about what should or should not be done. William kept his temper and refused to take sides in any argument, and so earned himself the title of William the Silent.

The rich Dutch merchants had flourished under the rule of Spain. At first, they could not make up their minds whether to support the rebellion or not. However, when the Spanish viceroy, the Duke of Alva, placed a new ten per cent tax on sales in 1558, they decided to back William with all their wealth.

Fighting between the Dutch and the Spaniards continued for the next ten years. William sold his gold and jewels to pay his soldiers. His brother, Prince John of Nassau, borrowed money by pledging his estates. Sometimes the Dutch won a battle, sometimes the Spaniards. The Dutch were victorious at Heiligerlie, only to be defeated a short time later at Jemmingen.

In 1567, William returned to Nassau to make plans and raise a new army. In September the following year, he crossed the River Maas with 18,000 foot soldiers and 7,000 cavalry. But the Spaniards refused to come against him in open battle. When his money came to an end, William had to send his soldiers home. The Duke of Alva was now, once again, master of the Netherlands.

In 1572, however, affairs took a new turn for William and the Dutch. William had given permission to some of his followers to act as privateers. These sea-rovers (known as Gueux de Mer, or the Sea Beggars) had fiercely attacked Spanish merchant ships, often treating the crews with great cruelty. But they had to use ports in England and East Friesland as their bases.

On 1st April, 1572, they attacked and seized the Dutch port of Britt, at the mouth of the River Maas. A little later they took Flushing, which stands at the entrance to another great waterway, the River Scheldt. Now the Sea Beggars had bases in their own country. Within three months of the capture of Britt, Amsterdam was the only city held by the Spaniards in the province of Holland.

The Duke of Alva now began to move with great force against the whole of Holland. At Malines he forced the inhabitants to surrender after three days of cruel butchery.

His son burnt and pillaged Zutphen and massacred the whole population of Naarden.

In the face of such cruelty, it would have been understandable if the Dutch had given in. But it was now that the true tenacity of the Dutch people began to show itself. The besieged city of Haarlem held out all through the winter of 1572/3, but had to surrender on 12th July, 1573. The citizens were spared, but all the soldiers were killed.

But at Alkmaar the tables were turned. The defenders opened the dykes and flooded all the countryside around, forcing the Spaniards to retreat. In October, the Sea Beggars defeated the Spanish Fleet on the Zuyder Zee, and took the admiral prisoner. The Spanish armies had not been paid for many months and began to mutiny.

King Philip recalled the Duke of Alva, and made Don Luis de Requesins the Viceroy in his place. Though the war went on, the two sides came together round the conference table. But they could not agree. The Dutch demanded the right to choose what religion they liked, the Spaniards insisted on a return to Roman Catholicism.

For the next six years, the fortunes of war swung backwards and forwards. During this time, the Dutch also split on the religious question. Those in the south, who had remained Catholics for the most part, became alarmed at the increase in in the number of Protestants, and they decided to form their own League for the Defence of the Catholic Religion. They also decided to remain under the protection of Spain.

Three weeks later, the northern provinces under William the Silent, formed a confederation, and the Union of Utrecht was signed by all the northern leaders, on 29th January, 1579. The confederation was run on the lines of a republic, with William the Silent as Stadtholder, or President, assisted by a parliament, known as the States-General (like the Dutch parliament today). At first, it was chiefly concerned with defending itself against the Spaniards.

The war with Spain was to continue for another thirty years but it almost came to an end in July 1584, when William was assassinated by a young French Catholic.

The struggle against the Spaniards had had its effect on William's private life. He was deeply in debt, his first wife, Anne of Saxony, left him and later divorced him; and, as Philip of Spain had declared him an outlaw, which meant that anyone had the right to kill him, he lived in constant fear of being assassinated.

His second wife was recovering from the birth of her baby, when a half-witted clerk employed by a Spanish merchant shot at him. The bullet went through his right ear and came out on the left of his jaw. The doctors, whose knowledge of medicine was nothing like that of our own day, did not know how to treat such a wound. They could only suggest pressing a pad of lint to the hole to stop the flow of blood. His wife insisted on doing this herself; she did so for several weeks without rest. Just as William began to recover, she died of exhaustion.

A room in the Frans Hals museum in Haarlem which gives a clear idea of the style of furnishing in the Netherlands in the sixteenth and seventeenth centuries

William had had many children by his two wives. His children needed a mother, so he married again. His new wife was Louise de Coligny, the daughter of a French admiral. For his protection, a large monastery at Delft was turned into a home for him. It was here that Balthazar Gérard appeared early in July 1584. Gérard told people who asked him that he was the only living son of a French Protestant family, all of whom had been massacred. This story had been thought up

20

by a priest who had convinced Gérard that he would be doing the Netherlands a great service if he killed William.

Everyone was taken in by Gérard's story; he was even allowed to visit the Prince in his bedroom. On 8th July he was seen in the corridors of the monastery and, when he was challenged, he said he was on his way to the church where William was to attend morning service. When someone pointed out that it was strange he had come in by the back door, Gérard replied, "My clothes are so old and worn, I am ashamed to use the main entrance." On being told this, William sent the young man some money to buy new clothes.

But, instead of buying clothes, Gérard bought two pistols. He also asked the Prince to give him a letter of safe conduct so that he could return to France without being stopped by Dutch officials. He was told to call for the letter.

Princess Louise, William's wife, was the first to see Gérard when he arrived on 10th July to receive this letter. She was startled by the strange look on the young man's face, and she ran to tell her husband of her alarm. William told her to be calm. "He's only a poor devil of a French refugee," he said. "An honest Protestant, who has suffered much for his religion."

The burgomaster (mayor) of Leeuwarden, Mijnheer van Uylenborch (the future father-in-law of Rembrandt, the great Dutch painter) had been having lunch with the Prince. As William was leading his guest from the dining-room along a corridor, he stopped at the foot of a staircase. Gérard had

21

hidden himself just here. He leapt out of his hiding-place and fired both pistols at the Prince. One bullet pierced William's lungs, the other his stomach. He fell on the steps, and the last words he spoke were, "Lord have mercy on my soul, and on these poor people."

The death of William, the Father of the Netherlands, made the position of the northern provinces desperate. William's eldest son was a prisoner of the Spaniards, so his second son, Maurice, though only seventeen, was elected Stadtholder. Maurice proved to be a great soldier, and he carried on the war with Spain. When he died, in 1625, he was succeeded by his younger brother, Frederick.

Frederick was Stadtholder for more than a quarter of a century. During this time the Dutch Republic passed through its Golden Age. After Frederick's death, the history of the Netherlands is again a history of wars—with the Spaniards, the English and the French.

By this time, the Netherlands had become a rich, powerful nation with a great empire. The Dutch were a great seafaring nation, whose navy and merchant fleet challenged the sea-might of England and France.

During the wars of Napoleon, the Netherlands were left alone until, in the winter of 1794/95, a large French army under General Charles Pichegru, swept into Holland. Somewhat strangely, the Dutch fleet, anchored at Texel, was captured by French cavalry which charged across the ice. The Stadtholder, Prince William V of Orange, fled to England

Children in church, dressed in national costume. Both the Catholic and Protestant religions flourish in the Netherlands

with his family, and the old government of the republic was completely replaced by a government on the French style. Napoleon made his brother, Louis, King of Holland, and the Dutch were forced to provide men and money for Napoleon's armies.

When Napoleon was defeated at Leipzig in 1813, French influence in the Netherlands melted away. The Prince of Orange, son of William V, hurriedly returned and was given the title of Sovereign Prince. In 1815, he was crowned as the first King of the Netherlands.

Fifteen years later, in 1830, the southern provinces rebelled. Their reasons for doing so were the higher taxes King William I demanded from them, and his attempts to make the French-

23

speaking provinces speak Dutch. A conference of the Great Powers—Russia, Prussia, Austria and Britain—met in London and, as a result of its discussions, the Netherlands was reorganised.

The Netherlands now consisted of the old republic, with the addition of a strip of land along the River Maas, which allowed the Dutch-speaking regions of Maastricht and Venlo to be included in the new country. The southern provinces were joined with Belgium, which was made a separate kingdom under King Leopold I, an uncle of Queen Victoria.

William I turned out to be an obstinate old man who would not change the rules he had made for the country, even when they were proved to be bad. In 1839, he abdicated and his son became King William II.

For the next nine years, the new king and his ministers had a difficult time saving their country from bankruptcy. The kind of government which had been drawn up when the Netherlands became a separate country was believed by many people, including the king, to be old-fashioned; a new kind of government replaced the old in October 1848.

Unfortunately, William II lived only a few more months. He died in March 1849. He was succeeded by his son, William III.

William III reigned for forty-one years. During his long reign the Netherlands went through a number of crises, but came out of each stronger than ever before. When William died in 1890, his daughter, Wilhelmina, became queen. But, as she was only ten years old, her mother ruled for her until she was eighteen.

The Netherlands did not take part in the First World War, which made the country unpopular with both sides from time to time. However, when the Germans invaded Belgium in 1914, and many Belgians fled to the safety of Holland, the Dutch looked after them very hospitably. At one time, there were more than one million Belgian refugees in the Netherlands.

By the 1830s, the Protestantism which had been the driving force of William the Silent's revolt against the Spaniards had lost much of its strength, as more and more people had changed back to Catholicism. At the end of the First World War, the Catholics and the Protestants were about equal in number, as they are today. (In 1971, 41.2 per cent were Protestant and 40.4 per cent were Roman Catholic, the rest representing other religions and non-believers.) This split between Catholics and Protestants has always coloured the political life of the Netherlands and has made the government of the country difficult from time to time. This is still true today.

The Dutch in the Second World War

The Dutch remained neutral in the First World War, and planned to do so again when it became clear that Hitler was going to take Germany into war once more. Immediately war broke out between Germany, Great Britain and France on 3rd September, 1939, the Dutch government declared its neutrality, but it is clear from what happened in the spring of 1940 that the Germans had always intended to invade the Netherlands, whether they were neutral or not.

The invasion began on 10th May, 1940, when the German armies rolled into the Netherlands and Belgium, just as they had into Denmark and Norway exactly a month earlier. Obviously, the Germans had planned this move many months ahead because they had planted spies in all the big cities. These Fifth Columnists, who were Germans with businesses in Holland and Dutchmen who were members of the Dutch National Socialist Party, which was run on exactly the same lines as Hitler's National Socialist (Nazi) Party, were armed and had radio transmitters and receivers, with which they were able to let the German High Command know the precise movements of the Dutch Army.

The Dutch Army was efficient and courageous, but had not the strength to hold back the hordes of German soldiers and tanks which poured over the frontier into the Netherlands in the dawn hours of that Friday morning. Though they had hoped they would never have to fight, the Dutch generals had prepared a plan of defence, which was to allow the Germans to come up to the so-called "waterline" formed in the east and south of the country by canals and rivers. The Germans would be halted on this line by the destruction of all the bridges.

Unfortunately, the German parachutists were able to capture some of the most important bridges before the Dutch could blow them up, and this enabled other German parachutists and ground forces to capture a number of airfields inside the "waterline". However, all the airfields except one, which the Germans captured in those first few hours, were retaken by the Dutch within twenty-four hours.

The Royal Dutch Air Force was very much under strength, though the Dutch government had made tremendous efforts to build it up in the year before the outbreak of war. It had about two hundred aircraft of all types, against which the Germans sent four or five times as many. Still, in the first two days of fighting the Air Force together with the anti-aircraft artillery shot down more than 180 German planes. But after that the air war was over, because Dutch losses were also very heavy.

It was this much greater air strength together with the vast masses of soldiers and tanks which the Germans sent against the Netherlands, which proved too much for the Dutch. All along the "waterline" there were fierce battles, and many thousands of Germans were killed. Dutch losses were much greater.

On 11th May, the Germans carried out an extremely heavy air-raid on the city of Rotterdam. When the German bombers flew back to their bases, the whole of the heart of the city was completely flattened. Not a single building was standing, except for the shell of the Groote Kerk, the city's chief church.

The bombing of Rotterdam showed that every other Dutch city could be destroyed in this way, if the Germans so wished. This, more than anything else, decided the Dutch High Command that they would have to surrender.

On 12th May, which was Whit Sunday, the Prime Minister warned Queen Wilhelmina that she and her government would soon have to leave the capital, The Hague. In the early hours of 13th May, the Commander-in-Chief decided that the move would have to be made as soon as possible. And, before midday, the Queen, Crown Princess Juliana, her husband, Prince Bernhard, and their two baby daughters, the Prime Minister and all his cabinet went to the Hook of Holland, where two British destroyers were waiting.

The Queen and her family boarded the first destroyer at once. While they were doing so, German aircraft attacked the ship, but fortunately did little damage. The cabinet went on board the second destroyer in the afternoon. Both ships reached

28

Queen Wilhelmina during the Second World War, in her study in London, reading "Underground" newspapers published by the Dutch resistance fighters

Britain safely, and the Queen and her ministers remained in London for the rest of the war. Princess Juliana was sent to the safety of Canada with her two babies, but Prince Bernhard stayed in England as Commander-in-Chief of the Free Dutch Air Force.

The Queen did not escape too soon. While she was on her way to the ship, German parachutists landed at the Royal Palace and at various ministries in The Hague, with instructions to capture the Royal Family and as many ministers as they could.

With Queen Wilhelmina, and Princess Juliana and her

Rotterdam today is typified by multi-storey buildings. This monument, entitled "Devastated City", is a constant reminder of the damage done to the city during the Second World War

babies safely out of the country, the Dutch High Command surrendered.

Every country which the Germans occupied during the war had its Resistance Movement. Some countries were slow in starting to resist, but the Netherlands resisted from the very first day. Within a couple of hours of the surrender being announced, a young man called Bernardus IJzerdraat distributed among his friends, copies of a message, written by hand, which said that he was organising a Resistance group, which he called *Geuzenactie*—"The Beggars' Action"—after the famous Sea-Beggars, who had caused the Spaniards so much trouble four hundred years earlier. Many of his friends joined IJzerdraat, and in October they drew up plans for an organisation which would cover the whole country. Unhappily, within a short time the Beggars' Action was betrayed and fifteen of its members were caught and shot by the Germans. They were the first Resistance victims. Before the war was over 2,000 members of the Resistance were to be shot.

(The brutality of the German treatment of the Dutch was sickening. During the occupation 105,000 Dutch Jews were murdered; between 10,000 and 20,000 Dutchmen died in concentration camps in Germany, and 4,000 in camps in Holland. Some 30,000 ordinary Dutchmen were starved to death; and, several years after the end of the war, 90,000 were still missing, most of whom were never found.)

Queen Juliana, the mother of the present Queen of the Netherlands

The German plan was to "Nazify" the Netherlands; that is, they intended to destroy the Dutch form of democratic government and replace it with the German form of government, which was a dictatorship—the rule of one man, in this case, Adolf Hitler. This plan actually included making the Netherlands into a province of Germany. Hitler sent Arthur Seyss-Inquart, an Austrian, who was sworn in as State Commissioner at the Hague on May 29th, to carry the plan through. Seyss-Inquart, one of the most cruel, but at the same time most able, of the Nazi leaders, lost no time in trying to "Nazify" the Netherlands.

At first he tried to win over the Dutch people. But it soon became clear that the Dutch did not want, or intend, to become Germans, and he began to treat them very harshly. Papers discovered after the war, showed that Hitler had made up his mind to move all the Dutch to eastern Europe if they refused to work with the Germans.

Everyone suffered intensely. There was already a shortage of food in Germany, and the Germans stole all the food they could lay their hands on in the Netherlands to send to their own people. Thousands of Dutchmen were hungry long before 1940 came to an end; but by 1944, tens of thousands had died of starvation.

But nothing that Seyss-Inquart could do, however cruel, would make the Dutch give in. The more harshly the Germans treated them, the more stubbornly they resisted.

Resistance takes many forms. "Underground" (secret)

newspapers were printed to disprove the German lies and keep up the spirits of the people. This was much more dangerous than it sounds. Anyone caught printing, giving out or reading one of these newspapers was liable to be shot, imprisoned or sent to a concentration camp or forced labour gang in Germany. But, despite the risks, the Dutch Resistance had more "underground" newspapers than any Resistance movement in other countries. By December 1943, 430,000 copies of these "illegal" news-sheets were sold every week.

Other Dutchmen formed organisations to resist the Germans in other ways. One of these organisations forged ration cards, which upset the Nazi rationing scheme. Another hid Dutchmen wanted by the Germans, especially Dutch Jews. Others carried out sabotage by blowing up factories making arms for the Germans, railways over which these arms and food were carried, electricity plants and bridges over canals.

The violent kind of Resistance naturally led to German soldiers being killed. To try to put a stop to it, Seyss-Inquart seized numbers of hostages, innocent Dutchmen who became known as "Candidates for Death"; for every German soldier killed, Seyss-Inquart ordered five of these hostages to be shot. Sometimes the executions were carried out in public, as a warning to other Dutchmen. But, no matter how cruelly the Germans treated them, they could not break the Dutchmen's courage and spirit.

Both the Roman Catholic and the Protestant Churches in the Netherlands joined in the Resistance in their own way.

Prince Bernhard

German soldiers were refused Holy Communion in Dutch churches, and priests and pastors encourage their congregations with warlike sermons. Many pastors and priests were shot or imprisoned.

The Dutch workers also played their part by coming out on strike. Only in two other countries—tiny Luxembourg, and Norway—was the strike used as a weapon of Resistance.

After the Russians began to drive the German armies back into Germany in the winter of 1942/43, and Field Marshal Montgomery defeated them in North Africa, it was clear to most people that Hitler would lose the war. This became even more certain when the Allies invaded France in June 1944.

Up to this time, the three largest Dutch Resistance groups which carried out sabotage had worked separately. In August 1944 they all joined together and, under Prince Bernhard's leadership, formed a Resistance Army, known as the Interior Forces.

The terrible winter of 1944/45 brought the climax to Dutch suffering. In the bitter cold, without heating and with scarcely any food, many thousands died. The lack of food lasted until the spring of 1945. Then, on the last day of April, the British Royal Air Force began to drop food by parachute.

By this time, the Allies had driven the Germans out of France, Belgium and the southern half of the Netherlands. Acting on orders from General Eisenhower, the Allied Supreme Commander, the Interior Forces in the north attacked the Germans from behind. This was too much for the Nazis. On 5th May they surrendered.

Throughout the war, the Dutch Government-in-Exile, in London, had kept in close contact with leaders in the Netherlands, and had drawn up plans to put their country back on its feet when peace came. On 23rd June, 1945, the Queen and the Dutch ministers returned and began to carry out their plans. Several years were to pass before life in the Netherlands was anything like normal once more.

The Lost Empire

It might well be thought that the Netherlands' continual struggle against the Spaniards for so many years would have occupied all the energies of the solid Dutch. Almost miraculously, however, they found time to make themselves into merchants, and not only merchants, but among the richest merchants in the world.

As courageous at sea as they were on land, they were a great seafaring nation. In 1602, they joined the company of great European explorers of the Far East and, a few years later, of the New World.

During the last half of the fifteenth century, the chief explorers of the Far East had been the Portuguese. In 1486 Bartolomeo Diaz had sailed down the west coast of Africa and rounded the Cape of Good Hope. His route was followed by Vasco da Gama in 1497, but da Gama went further up the east coast of Africa than Diaz. He also crossed the Indian Ocean, to Calicut, then a thriving trading centre on the

36

The Dutch have always been a seafaring nation. They are still famed for their shipping and the facilities provided by their docks. This is a view of the modern port of Rotterdam

south-east coast of India. He returned to Portugal in September 1499, his ship laden with a very valuable cargo of spices from the Far East.

For nearly one hundred years, the Portuguese were the chief suppliers of spices to Europe. Netherlands ships called at Portuguese ports and returned with cargoes of spices, which the Dutch merchants traded to northern Europe. Towards the end of the sixteenth century, however, Philip II of Spain closed the Portuguese ports to Netherlands ships, whereupon the Dutch said to themselves, "If the Portuguese can fetch spices from India, so can we." But they did even better than that. They sailed past India to Java, where the spices grew, and bought them direct from the Javanese more cheaply than they could from the traders of Calicut and Lisbon.

Portuguese traders had first explored the islands of the Indonesian archipelago, which consists of Sumatra, Java, Bali, Dutch Borneo, the Celebes, Dutch New Guinea and a host of smaller islands. Some Portuguese had stayed in the islands, but in the 1590s English and Dutch expeditions arrived and threw out the Portuguese. The Dutch were determined to have Indonesia for themselves. They fought the English there and defeated them.

In 1602, the Netherlands government set up the Dutch East India Company. The ships were owned by the Dutch merchants but, besides trading, they were required to do all they could to help their country in the struggle against Spain. They began by conquering the islands one by one, and ruling them in the name of the Netherlands government.

They turned the Portuguese out of Ceylon and Malacca, and the English out of the Spice Islands and Malaya, between 1613 and 1658. They also founded a colony at the Cape of Good Hope in 1652, which was the beginning of modern South Africa.

The Company reached the peak of its greatness in 1669. It then owned 150 trading ships and forty men-of-war, and employed 10,000 soldiers. In the eighteenth century its power

38

The harbour of Hoorn, once used by Dutch ships trading with the East Indies. In the background is the old town hall

began to decline. The struggle between the French and the English in India forced the Dutch out of Ceylon. By the end of the century, the Company was bankrupt, and was dissolved by the Netherlands government.

During the French occupation of the Netherlands between 1806 and 1810, the British seized the Netherlands East Indies from the Dutch.

There had been constant friction between the British and the Dutch over the centuries. This was more or less inevitable, because when you are a trading nation, as Britain and the

39

Netherlands both were, you have to have a navy to protect the sea-lanes along which your trading ships sail.

Britain had considered herself the Mistress of the Seas since the days of Queen Elizabeth I. When the Netherlands tried to displace her from first place, war broke out. The British and the Dutch went to war three times between 1652 and 1674. The first war lasted from 1652 to 1654, during the Protectorate of Oliver Cromwell.

The Dutch Admiral Martin von Trump tied a broom to the main-mast of his flag-ship as a signal to the British that he intended to sweep their navy from the seas. Two great sea battles were fought—there were no land battles in these wars—with neither side really winning, but in the third, which took place off the Dutch coast, Trump was severely defeated.

The second war broke out in the reign of Charles II. The Plague had greatly weakened the British navy and, in 1667, a Dutch fleet suddenly appeared in the River Thames, creating panic in London. After causing great damage, it sailed away. The third war (1672–1674) was very unpopular in England, and Charles was compelled to make peace with the Dutch.

There was no more fighting between Britain and the Netherlands until the English drove the Dutch out of the Netherlands East Indies in 1808. But when Napoleon was defeated at Waterloo, in 1815, the East Indies were returned to the Dutch.

Nineteen years after the foundation of the Dutch East India Company, the Dutch West India Company was formed.

40

This Company played a large part in settling Nieuwe Amsterdam, now called New York. It also took possession of the islands of Curaçao, Saba and St Martin's, in the West Indies. It was never so successful as the East India Company and it came to an end in 1674, though the Netherlands government kept its West Indies islands.

To return to the Dutch East Indies. In 1922, they became part of the kingdom of the Netherlands, and they remained so until the end of the Second World War.

During the Second World War the Japanese occupied all the islands forming Indonesia. Under Japanese encouragement, a political party—the Indonesian Nationalist Party—began to demand independence. In 1946, after the war was over, because of the tremendous damage the Germans had done to Holland, the Dutch government was not strong enough to resist the Nationalists' claims, though there was fighting between the Dutch and the Indonesians for some months. In December of that year, the independent Republic of Indonesia was born.

Of this great empire in East and West, all that remained were the West Indian islands of Curaçao, Bonaire, Amba, part of St Martin's, St Eustatius and Saba (now called the Netherlands Antilles), and Dutch Guiana (now called Suriname) on the northern coast of South America. Suriname became independent in 1975. The Netherlands Antilles is scheduled to become independent by 1990.

In the Country

Every town and city of the Netherlands seems to be wrapped in history, and the same is true of the countryside. Old customs are still followed and old costumes are still worn in many parts of this small country—in places which the modern world appears almost completely to have overlooked.

The Netherlands are divided into two major parts by the Rivers Rhine and Maas. It was the people north of this "waterline" who first became Protestants and who resisted all the attempts of the Spaniards to turn them back into Roman Catholics. The people of the south, who kept their Catholic faith, and who were brought into the kingdom of the Netherlands almost against their will, though decidedly Dutch, are not quite the same serious, determined people as the men of the north. This slight difference in personal character seems to have influenced the character of the countryside north and south of the "waterline."

But much more striking still is the difference between the provinces.

42

Dutch children wearing traditional local costumes

The Netherlands is divided into twelve provinces. When you remember that the area of Holland is only 34,830 square kilometres (13,500 square miles), the differences in character and customs as you pass from one province to another are really remarkable.

The northernmost province is Friesland whose people, the Frisians, speak their own language. This language is more like English than Dutch, and even Dutch people from other parts of the country cannot understand it. The Frisians are people of great independence. They have a motto: "Free is just another name for Frisian."

43

A typical dairy farming scene in Holland

Friesland is the great dairy province of the Netherlands. Its cheese, butter, milk and famous black-and-white cattle are exported to many places.

Quite a large area of Friesland is formed by land reclaimed from the sea—the North-east Polder, as it is called. What probably strikes a visitor most about the North-east Polder is its wide, straight roads, which have none of the bends of the old farmland roads. Straight as the dykes themselves, they are broken only by clusters of farmhouses. Broad fields of yellow mustard, bronze flax, green alfalfa and brown barley form the countryside into a colourful chequers board.

44

On the western edge of the polder is the little town of Urk, once an island in the Zuyder Zee. Because it was cut off from other communities not far away, it developed its own way of life, traditions and costumes.

When the polder joined it to the mainland in 1942, the people decided that this was no reason for them to make any changes in how they lived. They will not allow cars inside their town, and they are such strict Protestants that they forbid people to ride their bicycles on Sundays.

They still wear their traditional costumes, too. The women wear a corsage of light-blue material, covered with pieces of chamois leather, to prevent wear, and stiffened with whale-bones. A broad yoke of flowered silk is worn over this. On the back of the head goes a white bonnet. Garnets are worn around the neck and gold ornaments in the ears.

The men wear black wooden shoes, thick black socks, black pantaloons fastened about the knee, and a round black hat. Sometimes a silver belt-buckle and gay red-and-white striped shirt brighten up this sombre costume.

Traditional costumes are still worn in the country districts in many parts of the Netherlands. Usually one sees them on market days, Sundays and festivals. The women's head-dresses can be very beautiful. Some, however, are merely simple lace caps.

Off the Frisian coast are the islands of Texel, Vlieland, Terschelling and Ameland. All have long and wide stretches of sandy beach on their northern sides. They have not yet been

The River Linge in Gelderland

spoiled by luxury hotels and amusement parks. Here you can have a lazy, quiet holiday in a simple hotel, or on one of the many camping-sites.

The province of Groningen has not quite the charm of Friesland but it, too, is a flourishing agricultural region. It has rich arable and pasture lands, and the prosperity of the farmers can be seen in their firm, solid houses. About fifty mediaeval churches have been preserved, complete with their squire's pew and coat-of-arms, and monuments recalling the past.

Drenthe province consists mostly of worked out peat-beds. It could be very ugly, but the local people have covered up the disused diggings with woods. There is a legend that a race of giants, known as Hunen, once lived here. The legend is based on the fact that a number of prehistoric barrows, dating from about 2000 B.C. called *Hunebedden*, are dotted about the province.

The province of Limburg has long rolling hills—the Netherlands are not entirely flat—woods, running streams, moorlands and meadows. The people, though Dutch, are more like the Walloons of northern Belgium. They are happy and full of fun, and seize on any excuse to hold a feast or a carnival.

Gelderland is the garden province of the Netherlands. Its

The largest "Hunebed" (prehistoric burial site) in Drenthe

countryside has gentle slopes, many streams and old trees. Beautiful gardens can be seen everywhere.

The province of North Brabant is the great industrial region of the Netherlands. At Eindhoven the famous Philips organisation, known throughout the world for its electrical products, has its headquarters. But dotted about the province, too, are a number of castles which look as if they were built for Sleeping Beauty.

The Evoluon—a permanent scientific exhibition established by Philips of Eindhoven

Castle Bouvigne in North Brabant

North Brabant is the largest Dutch province, along with Gelderland—they have exactly the same area. The smallest is Utrecht, though its capital city (of the same name) is the fourth largest city in the Netherlands. It is probably the most varied province, with its numerous modern luxury hotels and its many villages where the people wear local costume and live according to old traditions.

But no matter where you go in the Netherlands, you will see windmills. Though there are now only one thousand left of the ten thousand there once were, they seem to be a part of the Dutch countryside. Each region of the country has its own type of windmill. In the past, their main job was draining the land; now they are used to generate and store electricity.

The millers signal to one another with the sails of their

49

Drainage mills which are mainly used to raise water from one level to the next

mills when they are not turning. Placed in certain positions they indicate the birth of a child, a wedding or a death. Without the windmills, the Netherlands would not be the same place.

End

Schools and Universities

The Dutch are among the best educated people in the world. This is partly because they have always been more interested in education for all than most other peoples, and partly because for the last fifty years of the nineteenth century education was one of the chief subjects for argument between the political parties.

As we have seen, the struggle against Spain was really a struggle between Protestants and Catholics. William of Orange (the Silent) who may be regarded as the Father of the Netherlands, always insisted, however, that anyone living in Holland could practise any religion he chose. He declared this first in 1564, but it was repeated many times through the centuries by various governments.

Roman Catholicism did not disappear when Spain was at last turned out of the country. In fact, it remained quite strong, though Roman Catholics were not allowed the same privileges as the Protestants. It seemed that though every man could practise whatever religion he chose, this did not make Protestants and Catholics equal; and since the leaders

51

The parents of these schoolchildren can choose whether they wish to send their children to private or State schools but they must send them to school, at least until they are sixteen years old

were always Protestants, they naturally made sure that the Catholics did not have quite the same rights of citizenship as they had. These differences were officially brought to an end in 1798, but the fact is that Dutch politics are founded on religion. The three largest parties are the Catholic People's Party, and the Labour and Anti-revolutionary Parties, these last two representing Protestant views.

Roman Catholics everywhere have always insisted on having their own schools. In Protestant countries this means that the Catholic schools must be "private" schools as distinct from State schools. But the picture in the Netherlands has always been slightly different, because the stricter Protestants

52

have always insisted on having their own "private" schools as well.

The Netherlands government first took an interest in education in 1806, during the French occupation, when it proposed that all "private" schools should be open to Catholics and Protestants. Both Protestants and Catholics resisted this but, after a long struggle, it was agreed that *all* "private" schools should receive financial help from the State.

The date on this building in the centre of Nijmegen is 1605, but the town has more modern parts too, including the university which was founded in 1923

There have always been more "private" schools in the Netherlands than State schools. For example, there are 2,523 State primary schools with 425,000 pupils and double that number, 5,172, "private" primary schools with 1,065,000 pupils. The "private" schools receive exactly the same financial help from the government as the State schools. Except for two or three secondary schools for girls only, boys and girls go to the same schools.

There is practically no one in the Netherlands who cannot read or write. Children have been compelled to attend school from the age of six since 1900. Until just before the Second World War, Dutch boys and girls had to remain at school until they were thirteen. Now the school-leaving age is sixteen, but large numbers go on to secondary schools of one kind or another, where they stay until they are eighteen.

There are six universities in the Netherlands. The three oldest—Leyden, founded in 1575, the most famous, Groningen, founded in 1614, and Utrecht in 1636—are State universities, at which anyone of any religion or no religion at all, may study. Amsterdam has two universities, one of which belongs to the city council. The other, the Free University, is for Protestants only. The sixth university is a Roman Catholic one, founded at Nijmegen in 1923.

Besides these universities, there are a number of colleges for advanced learning in economics, agriculture and technical training, and a college for medicine at Rotterdam. With such a large system of education, many teachers are required, and there are more than ninety teacher-training colleges. This is for a total population of 14,200,000 Dutchmen, whereas Britain has 149 teacher training colleges for a total population of 55,047,000; or less than twice as many for four times the number of people.

The Dutch have set a very high standard not only in their universities, where it is exceptionally high, but also in their schools. From the very first day at their primary school boys and girls are expected to work very hard right through to the day that they leave school, whether they leave their primary school at sixteen, or their secondary school at eighteen. Since 1971, students have sat on university governing bodies. The Dutch are, in fact, among the best, if they are not *the* best, educated people in the world.

A view of Leyden, the home of the oldest university in the Netherlands, founded in 1575

How the Dutch Live

The Dutch have a saying: "God created the world, but the Dutch made the Netherlands." In so far as they have reclaimed a very large part of their land from the sea, this saying is certainly true. And it is this constant struggle with the sea that has made the Dutchman the strong, solid character that he is.

His ceaseless battle to stop the sea from taking back the land he has won from it, has given the Netherlander a serious view of life, which has been strengthened by the stern beliefs of his Calvinist Protestant religion. About two-fifths of the people are strict Protestant, about two-fifths are Roman Catholic and the remainder belong to no church. But as a leading Roman Catholic once said, "In Holland, the Roman Catholics are Calvinistic, too!" In consequence, the Dutchman is serious, hardworking, law-abiding, helpful and kind, but without any great sense of humour.

Cyclists crossing one of Amsterdam's many canals. Bicycles are a very popular form of transport in all parts of the Netherlands

He is also a great family man. In countries like France, Italy and Spain, men spend much time in cafés and bars, but the Dutchman stays at home.

The average Dutchman gets up early and rides to work on his bicycle. (It is probably true to say that every Dutch man, woman and child rides a bicycle. Even the Queen and other members of the Royal Family may be seen riding bicycles in the countryside around the palace at Soestdijk, some sixteen kilometres—ten miles—or so, east of Amsterdam.) He takes sandwiches with him, usually in a little briefcase, works hard until about five o'clock in the afternoon, and goes home to an early dinner, between six and seven o'clock.

57

The Royal Palace of Soestdijk

After dinner, he stays at home. First, he reads his evening newspaper, which will have been delivered a short time before dinner. The evening newspapers are considered much more important than the morning editions. They are larger and they carry much more news. The Dutchman generally does not put it down until he has read it from cover to cover.

When he has finished with the newspaper, he may watch television, listen to the radio, play chess or play a musical instrument. Or he may do nothing but sit. More often than not someone will call, for the Dutchman keeps open house, and he expects his friends to drop in on him without invitation, just as he will sometimes drop in on friends.

Because he passes so much of his time in his house, he spends a good deal of money on it, and especially on those parts where he receives his friends. The living-room has knick-knacks of all kinds. It is usually the front room of the house overlooking the street and, as the curtains are not drawn, the passer-by has a good view of the room, the family and its guests. To draw the curtains would be to suggest that something was going on in the room that was not quite nice.

Outside nearly every Dutch house stands a motorcar. This is the most important thing to a Dutchman after his house, because it shows how successful he has been at making a living for himself. As the country is small, and the distances between one place and the next are not very great, most cars are used only at weekends. From Monday to Friday they are covered by a kind of tent. On Friday, the housewife will remove the tent and wash and polish the car so that it is shining and ready for the next two days' excursions.

Most Dutchwomen wash at least their downstairs windows —and, if they live in a city, the pavement in front of their house—every day. Every house, too, will have its pots of flowers in the windows. And if there should be a garden, even if it is only the size of a pocket handkerchief, it will be full of flowers.

When you consider the Dutchman's serious nature, this great love of flowers may seem surprising. But it may be connected with another of his great interests—painting. There are comparatively few Dutchmen who are unable to understand and appreciate painting. The same is also true of music. Even after the tourists have left at the end of the season, the museums and art galleries are always crowded by the Dutch people themselves. Every town of any size has its own symphony orchestra; and most villages will have at least a brass band.

The Amsterdam concert-hall—home of the famous Netherlands Concert-Gebouw Orchestra

The Dutch are among the most polite people in Europe. If a Dutchman walks into a barber's, or the compartment of a train, he will say good morning or good afternoon, even though he may not know a single person there—and everyone will return his greeting. At a party or a business meeting, he will introduce himself to each person by a quick hand-shake, saying his surname.

It is the height of bad manners for a Dutchman to be late for an appointment. Should this happen he will make long, profuse apologies. He also takes you at your word. The casual, "Next time you are near by, do drop in," is a firm invitation to visit.

Sometimes when two English friends go out for an evening's entertainment, each will pay his own way. This is called a "Dutch treat" or "going Dutch," and it is well named. If you say to a Dutchman, "Let's have lunch together," he will expect to pay for his own meal. If, however, he wants you to be his guest, he will say so—"Will you be my guest for lunch?" or "May I invite you to lunch?" Then he will pay for you, too. (He will pay in Dutch florins, or guilders, each of which is made up of one hundred cents.)

It would be wrong to suppose from all this, however, that the Dutchman is a dull fellow who cannot enjoy himself, or that because he places so much importance on his home he has no social life outside it. He can, and does, enjoy a glass of beer or a nip of Dutch gin and a short chat at a café or bar at about five o'clock, on his way home from work; and few other people

A "rijsttafel" in an Amsterdam Indonesian restaurant

in Europe celebrate birthdays like the Dutch. On each anniversary of each member of the family all friends are welcome to "drop in" from ten o'clock in the morning until late in the evening to toast the health of the person whose birthday it is, and to take light refreshments.

The Dutch like their food. Ordinary Dutch cooking is simple without any fancy trimmings, and is intended to be nourishing. On the other hand, the old colonists (who lived for a time in Indonesia and then returned to the Netherlands to retire) have introduced many exciting Indonesian dishes into the Dutchman's menu, such as *nasi goreng* (fried rice) or *nasi bami* (fried noodles) eaten with choice pieces of meat,

62

shrimp, chicken and so on. The most elaborate Indonesian meal is called a *rijsttafel*, which starts off with a dish of plain steamed rice. This is followed by from fifteen to fifty dishes each one more tasty than the last. If you go through the whole meal, you will want to sleep for several hours afterwards, which is what most Dutchmen do.

For breakfast, the Dutch eat bread or rolls with thin slices of Dutch cheese, prepared meats and sausage, a boiled egg, jam or honey, and drink coffee, tea or chocolate. Lunch consists of more bread, cold meats, cheese and jam.

Dinner is the most important meal of the day and is eaten quite early. It consists of soup, a main dish and dessert. Two of the most famous of Dutch soups are a thick pea soup often served with pieces of smoked sausage, cubes of pork fat, pig's

Eating salted herrings the traditional way. Sometimes they are sold from barrels in the streets in Amsterdam and the people stop and eat them in the way that people in other countries buy and eat ice-creams

knuckle and slices of brown or white bread; and a thin, clear soup full of vegetables, vermicelli and tiny meat balls.

The Dutch eat large amounts of vegetables and meat. They also have many varieties of fish such as salted herrings, whiting, sole, shrimp, mussels and smoked eel, all of which are obtained from Dutch rivers and coastal waters.

There is one particularly interesting dish, called *hutspot*, which is eaten by Dutchmen all over the world. The town of Leyden was besieged by the Spaniards for nearly a year in 1573/74, and when it was at last freed on 3rd October, 1574, the starving people were given *hutspot*. It is a stew of potatoes, carrots and onions served with lean beef. A little of it goes a long way.

The Dutch at Work and at Play

The Dutch have always been a seafaring nation, like the British, whose rivals they were for some time. Their sailors ventured far afield to the countries of the east and returned with spices, diamonds and many other kinds of rich merchandise. By the beginning of the sixteenth century, Dutch merchants had formed a very flourishing trade with Scandinavia, Russia and what is now northern Germany. It was to increase this trade and extend it to other parts of Europe that the Dutch East India Company was formed in 1602.

The founding of the Company was the beginning of the Dutch Empire, and this made the Netherlands richer than ever. Though not the capital of the country, Amsterdam has always been the chief city of the Netherlands, and the shrewd merchants of Amsterdam soon made their city the great money market of Europe.

Antwerp, in Belgium, had been Europe's great diamond centre in the Middle Ages, because it was the first port of call for ships from India. But, when the Spaniards conquered Belgium in 1576, many of the Antwerp diamond experts fled to Amsterdam. They were joined less than a hundred years later by many cutters of gems who had to flee their own countries because of religious persecution. At that time, diamond fields were discovered in Brazil, and most of the uncut stones were sent to Amsterdam to be cut and polished. But it was the discovery of diamonds in South Africa in the second half of the nineteenth century that made Amsterdam the diamond centre of the world.

Apart from the activities of the Amsterdam merchants, who made large fortunes buying and re-selling goods from all parts of the world, and from diamonds, the chief occupation of the Dutch was agriculture. It still is.

On the other hand, the Dutch were not slow in seeing the advantages of industry. Unfortunately for the Netherlands, there are very few minerals to be found there. Even coal was in short supply. However, the government was prepared to help import the necessary minerals, and soon the country could boast industry, as well as agriculture.

The chief industries are shipbuilding—which is the largest—textiles, paper-making and pottery. About half a century ago, coal was discovered in Limburg and, as a result, chemical, iron and steel industries were set up. Another very important industry is the making of electrical and radio equipment. The Dutch electrical firm of Philips is world famous.

Though agriculture employs a very large part of the

Tulip beds at Keukenhof

population, there are few large farms. Only one in a hundred is bigger than fifty hectares (125 acres) and most are about ten hectares (twenty-five acres). The chief crops are wheat, barley, rye, oats and sugar beet.

With the exception of Switzerland, the Netherlands have more cattle per hectare or acre than any other country in Europe. Cattle and pigs are reared in great numbers, both to feed the Dutch themselves and for export. But perhaps the best known of all the dairy products are the Dutch cheeses such as Edam and Gouda, which have been famous for hundreds of years.

Without doubt, the most famous of all the products of the Netherlands' soil is the tulip. Tulips were first brought to

67

Holland from Turkey in 1559, and the Dutch went mad about them. So much, in fact, that they were said to be suffering from "tulipomania". Tulipomania reached its height in 1637 when as much as 2,600 guilders (more than most people would earn for several weeks' work) was paid for a single bulb. But these prices did not last long, and when "the bubble burst", many thousands of Dutchmen went bankrupt. The Dutch introduced the tulip into England in the latter half of Queen Elizabeth I's reign.

The bulbfields of Holland are one of the country's great sights in April and May, when the flowers are in bloom. Many thousands of tourists visit them and excursions are arranged. It is impossible to describe the glorious carpets of colour. For example, at the 26-hectare (60-acre) Keukenhof Gardens at Lisse, as many as five million bulbs bloom all at the same time.

The Dutch work very hard and have made their country very prosperous. But, though their outlook on life is solemn and they are so hardworking, they also like to enjoy themselves in their leisure time.

Because there is so much water in the Netherlands, water-sports, naturally, are extremely popular. There are many beautiful beaches around the coasts; they are all broad, and free of pebbles and stones. Perhaps the best known resort is Scheveningen (a suburb of The Hague) because it has the biggest hotels and the greatest choice of amusements, as well as a beach with golden sand.

Many Dutch, however, reckon the beaches on the islands which guard the entrance to the Zuyder Zee to be the best. Their natural beauty has not been spoiled by large hotels and amusements and they provide the best swimming, though you have to be careful to obey the regulations and keep within the limits set by the beach authorities. This is because of the treacherous currents some way out from the shore, which can sweep away the strongest swimmers. There is only one snag about these island beaches. Though the sun may be shining brilliantly, very often a cold wind blows across them which may make you keep your jacket or a cardigan on over your swim-suit.

Next to swimming, boating is the most popular pastime in

Loosdrecht, a popular harbour for yachtsmen

The popular holiday resort of Scheveningen

the Netherlands. Sailing-boats glide up and down the canals and on the lakes which are dotted about the countryside south and west of Amsterdam. The canals are often hidden by the fields of grain through which they flow. If you are a visitor in a motorcar, you may be quite puzzled when you see sails which seem to be crossing dry land.

Foreigners are often amused by the Dutchman and his bicycle. But again, the flatness of the countryside makes cycling a pleasant leisurely pastime. Often, if the wind is at your back, you may not have to pedal at all.

The Dutch claim that they invented golf, though everyone else "knows" that it was first played at St Andrews, in Scotland. There are eighteen first-class golf courses scattered throughout the country; for a country the size of the Netherlands, this is a lot, and shows how popular the game is.

The most popular team game is soccer, which the Dutch call *voetbal*. There are some teams, such as Ajax (Amsterdam) and Feyenoord (Rotterdam) which are as famous throughout Europe as Chelsea or Real Madrid.

With all the rivers, canals and lakes, in winter there are great opportunities for skating. Just as "every Dutchman rides a bicycle", so "every Dutchman skates". Not every winter has such low temperatures that skating is possible all the time, but every three or four years there is severe cold for months on end. When this happens, a great race, known as the Eleven Towns Race, is held. Prizes are given not only for the fastest skaters, but to all those who have the strength to finish the course, which is between forty-eight and sixty-four kilometres (thirty and forty miles) long.

Except for skating, the Dutch do not go in for much outdoor sport in winter. They are very keen on judo, however, and every city of any size has its sport academy or academies, where judo experts give instruction to crowded classes.

The countries of southern Europe have many public holidays

71

**Skaters taking part
in the Eleven
Towns Race**

and carnivals. The Netherlands also has its holidays, with their special customs, though not so many.

The Dutch do not make much of Christmas. Instead they celebrate 5th December, the feast of St Nicholas, when they exchange presents and eat a good deal of marzipan in every shape and form, as well as spiced ginger biscuits, spiced cakes in the form of animals and figures, tall chocolate letters in the shape of an initial S, and *banketletter*—initials made of pastry filled with almond paste.

In every town St Nicholas, with a white beard like Santa Claus, but dressed in a long red robe, a red and gold bishop's mitre on his head, and a bishop's crook in his hand, drives through the streets accompanied by his Moorish servant, called Zwarte Piet (Black Peter). As he goes, he gives sweet-meats to the children who greet him.

The Dutch do have a tree at Christmas. But the festival is a quiet family affair, with the children gathering round the tree to listen to father reading the story of the first Christmas from the New Testament.

The Dutch also celebrate Easter and Whitsun, but the most important other holiday is the Queen's Birthday on 30th April. All the large cities are decorated with the Royal Standard and with clusters of orange-coloured balls in honour of the House of Orange, of which the Queen is the head.

St. Nicholas and
Black Peter

**The Alkmaar
cheese market**

Since the Second World War, 5th May, Liberation Day—
the day on which the Germans in the Netherlands surrendered
to the Allies—has also been a public holiday.

Besides these national holidays, many Dutch towns and
villages have their own traditional celebrations. For example,
in several towns and villages on Ascension Day the inhabitants go out into the surrounding countryside *dauwtrappen*—
"treading the dew". On Midsummer Eve, 24th June, the
people of Laren, twenty-five kilometres (eighteen miles)
south-east of Amsterdam, go in procession to the woods just
outside the town, and assemble in the Old Cemetery where
many centuries ago pagan sacrifices were carried out.

Wherever you may be in the Netherlands, market days are

74

always special days, but the most interesting are the cheese markets at Alkmaar and Gouda. The Alkmaar cheese market was started in 1571 as a special privilege. Every Friday from late April to the end of September, porters in ancient costumes go down to the quay where Edam and Gouda cheeses arrive in barges. The cheeses are thrown ashore to the porters, who never fail to catch them. They are loaded into barrows and taken to the nearest square, which is hung with international flags. The buyers cluster around them and examine them, and then begin to make their bids. As they do so, they clap each others' hands. The highest price is chalked up on a board.

The porters, or to give them their correct title, the Guild of Cheese Carriers, then put the cheeses on flat-bottomed wooden floats, which have curved shafts to which a harness is attached.

The Alkmaar porters in their Guild uniforms

The carriers put the harness on their shoulders and carry the cheeses to the weigh-house, where they are weighed and marked for the buyer.

The Gouda cheese market is held on Thursday mornings from May until the middle of September in the beautiful old town hall. All those who visit the market may taste the cheeses, and watch a film showing how they are made.

Some of the fishing-ports have their ancient local customs, too. The most stirring is the first departure of the herring-boats in the spring. During the weeks before, the herring casks have been scrubbed and the luggers and trawlers painted and made ship-shape. On sailing-day the villages are all decorated

Herring-boats in harbour; note the barrels for the herrings in the foreground, and the fishing nets on the cart

with flags and bunting, and bets are made on which boat will be first back with its load of herrings. The first cask to be landed is presented to the Queen, and there is great competition among the fishermen for this honour.

Throughout the summer various places put on ancient traditional sports. In the north, there are competitions in the ball-game known as *kaatsen*, and archery competitions, while in the south there are banner-waving displays. In these last, huge banners are whirled about the performer's head and body in fantastic patterns.

Finally, since the end of the Second World War, the *Holland Festival* has been held every year between 15th June and 8th July. This festival is similar to the famous Edinburgh and Salzburg festivals. Concerts are given by the best Dutch and foreign orchestras, theatre companies put on classical and modern plays, and ballet companies give performances of old and new ballets. Though most of the entertainments are staged in and around Amsterdam, Scheveningen and The Hague, some take place in smaller towns and cities throughout the country.

Certainly the Dutch know how to enjoy themselves.

The Cities

Almost a thousand years ago, some fishermen came ashore
with their boats on a sandbank where the River Amstel flows
into the River IJ (pronounced *eye*), which was then an
estuary of the Zuyder Zee. Within a few years others joined
them and, within three hundred years, the village they had
founded had become the most important trading centre of the
Netherlands; and, indeed, one of the most important in
Europe. By 1482, it had grown into a sizeable city, protected
by a wall.

The name, meaning the Dam on the Amstel, was early

**A typical
gabled house
in Amsterdam**

Amsterdam's Spiegelsgracht, so named because the canal mirrors the houses, bridges and trees ("spiegel" is the Dutch for mirror)

changed from Amsteldam to Amsterdam. When, during the period of Spanish rule in the sixteenth century, the great port of Antwerp lost much of its trade, this trade moved to Amsterdam, which reached even higher peaks of importance. Its ships were to be seen in every port in the world, and its flag flew over trading companies in every continent.

Amsterdam is sometimes called the Venice of the North. If you look at a street plan of the city you will see why. Four semi-circles of canals ring the heart of Amsterdam. The first (inner) canal began as the moat which ran outside the wall of the city. As the city grew outside the walls, in time, a second, a third and a fourth ring of canals was added.

79

These canals made it possible to bring ships into the heart of the city and unload them there. Many of the old houses whose upper storeys were used as warehouses for the vast loads of tea, spices, silks, furs and other exotic things, still exist. From their top-most gables the beams for the pulleys by which the cargoes were hoisted into store still jut out; only the ropes are missing.

The canals, with streets running on either side of them, and crossed by others, give the city its unique charm. Though barges instead of gondolas glide up and down them, and the architecture of the houses and buildings is quite different from that of Venice, Amsterdam has a beauty which equals that of the Italian city.

The centre point of Amsterdam is the Dam Square. Here is the huge Royal Palace. It was built to replace the old town hall, but was turned into a palace by King Louis Bonaparte in 1808. The Nieuwe Kerk—the New Church—which was begun in 1408, is to its right. Though The Hague is the capital of the Netherlands where parliament meets and the government ministries are situated, Amsterdam has always been the most important city. The rulers of Holland are not crowned, they are "inaugurated". Every ruler since William I (1813) to Queen Beatrix (1980) has been inaugurated in the New Church.

The Royal Palace is only used on formal occasions today. The Queen lives in the country at the palace of Soesdijk, near Utrecht.

Kalverstraat, Amsterdam's most important shopping street, leads out of the Dam Square and, only a short distance away, across the square, at No. 4 Jodenbreestraat is the house where the great master painter, Rembrandt, lived from 1639 to 1658.

The Netherlands have produced many famous painters. Frans Hals, whose picture *The Laughing Cavalier* is one of the best-known pictures in the world, lived and worked in Haarlem between 1580 and 1666. Before him were Pieter Brueghel the Elder and his two sons, Pieter the Younger and Jan, whose pictures of skating scenes and scenes from rustic life are as famous as any of Hals' paintings. And he was followed by Albert Cuyp, Jacob van Ruysdael, Jan Vermeer, Pieter de Hoogh and others. But, without doubt, the greatest of them all was Rembrandt.

Most visitors to Amsterdam go to the Rijksmuseum and look at the fabulous collection of Rembrandt's pictures, particularly the huge one called *The Night Watch*, and one of a group of men called *The Syndics*. These two pictures reveal the seventeenth-century men of Holland's Golden Age, the wise and solemn councillors, the rich merchants.

As you explore Amsterdam, you are almost certain to hear one of the famous street organs. Pushed from street to street by a team of husky men, they pour out a torrent of sound—drums, pipes, cymbals and so on, all mixed up in a fantastic noise. Nowhere else in the world can such street organs be found.

Amsterdam is still one of the great ports of the world, and

One of
Amsterdam's
famous street
organs

the shipyards across the IJ are among the busiest in the world. As well as shipping, modern Amsterdam is famous for its diamond industry. All but ten per cent of the world's diamonds pass through Amsterdam. The diamond-cutters and polishers welcome visitors. They demonstrate to them "how it is all done" on glass dummies, and show them priceless collections of the gems, securely locked away in specially constructed show-cases.

THE HAGUE AND DELFT

The Hague is an aristocrat of a city. Compared with Amsterdam or Rotterdam, which are no mean cities themselves, The Hague is always on its dignity.

In Dutch, the official name of The Hague is *'s Gravenhage*,

82

which means the Count's Hedge. It has been called this from early in the thirteenth century, when the Counts of Holland had a hunting-lodge in a small woodland village called the *Hage*, or Hedge.

The centre of interest in The Hague is the Ridderzaal, or Knights' Hall, which is the oldest building in the city. On the third Tuesday in September, Queen Beatrix drives in a golden coach to the Ridderzaal and, amid great pageantry, opens the new session of parliament.

Perhaps of equal interest is the Mauritshuis, a seventeenth-century mansion now an art museum, which has a wonderful collection of Dutch masters, including several Rembrandts, and Vermeer's most famous picture *View of Delft*.

But The Hague is, first and foremost, a city of civil servants—

The Peace Palace, the seat of the International Court of Justice at The Hague

The Ridderzaal,
The Hague

respectable and a little dull. Still, if you ever find yourself
there, you should also visit the miniature city of Madurodam.
Madurodam consists of models of typical buildings, industry
and transport from all over the Netherlands on a scale of
one-quarter life-size.

Delft is about twelve kilometres (eight miles) east of Rotterdam, and nine kilometres (six miles) from The Hague.
There is no other city like Delft in the Netherlands, in Europe

84

or in the world. Every street is lined with mediaeval houses which have all their charm and beauty still. When you go to Delft, do not tour the city lolling comfortably in one of the many water-taxis which glide up and down the web of canals. If you do, you will miss much of Delft's beauty. Go on foot, so that you have time to pause and look and wonder.

Vermeer lived and painted in Delft all his life, and nowadays a colony of modern Dutch painters have made their home there. The greatest Dutch scholar of all time, Hugo de Groot, better known as Grotius, was born here, and is buried in the fourteenth-century New Church.

William the Silent made Delft his headquarters during his struggle with the Spanish Duke of Alva and lived in the convent of St Agatha, now known as the Prinsenhof. It was

Making Delft pottery

A canal in Delft, the home of the famous blue and white pottery

here that he was assassinated; and you can still see the holes in the plaster made by the bullets fired at him.

The Prinsenhof is regarded as the cradle of Dutch liberty. Part of it is used as a museum telling the story of the Liberation of the Netherlands from 1568 to 1648.

But Delft is perhaps most widely known for the beautiful blue and white earthenware that has been produced here for several centuries. The early tiles are much sought after as antiques, and fetch very high prices. In the Lambert van Meerten Museum, a beautiful old mansion with beamed rooms, there is the finest collection of Delft pottery in the world.

86

It seems that every Dutch city has played an important part in the history of the Netherlands at some time or another. Utrecht is no exception. It was the signature here in 1579 of the Union of Utrecht which laid the foundations for the later Kingdom of the Netherlands.

Utrecht, some forty kilometres (twenty-five miles) southeast of Amsterdam, is the fourth largest city in the Netherlands. It historical past now tends to get hidden by the Royal Netherlands Industrial Fair, which is held twice a year in the imposing modern building which was finished in 1970. The fairs get larger every time they are held, and are very important to the life of the country.

LEYDEN

Leyden has a number of claims to fame. It was here that William of Orange founded a university in 1575 which quickly became a meeting-place for scholars from all parts of Europe. It is still the Netherlands' chief university and is specially famous for its medical school.

Rembrandt was born here, so was another famous Dutch artist, Jan Steen.

In the Middle Ages, it was the centre of the cloth trade in Europe. And it was a group of Englishmen, who fled from religious persecution in their own country, who settled first in Amsterdam, then moved to Leyden, and then became the Pilgrim Fathers.

A view of the Leyden
university

From 1573 to October 1574, the city was besieged by the
Spaniards. The sufferings of the citizens were great; the food
situation became so desperate that the burgomaster (mayor)
offered his own body as food. Six thousand men, women and
children died of starvation before the siege was raised.

Strangely, though Leyden is an inland city, relief came from
the sea. The Dutch fleet sailed "overland" from lake to lake,
breaking a different dyke each night, so that it could advance
again next morning.

The Spaniards fled from the city on 3rd October, 1574;
every year since then, bread and herrings have been distri-

buted on that day to commemorate this great event in Dutch history.

ROTTERDAM

Rotterdam is to the province of South Holland what Amsterdam has been to North Holland. Situated on the deltas of the Rhine and the Maas (Meuse), it has become, since the Second World War, the largest sea-port in the world. More shipping passes in a year through its many harbours than through all the ports of France.

Old Rotterdam—the city hall

Rotterdam rebuilt

Much of Rotterdam's modern development has been made possible by the German air attack on the city on 14th May, 1940. In a few hours' bombing the whole jumbled ancient centre of Rotterdam was flattened to the ground. More than 30,000 houses, shops, churches and schools were destroyed.

Four days after the catastrophe, the Rotterdammers began work on plans for a new city. Gradually, over the years, a new city of concrete, steel and glass has come into being. Dutch architects have always been among the more adventurous in Europe. Though the lover of ancient buildings may dislike the modern styles of building, it cannot be denied that the new Rotterdam is one of the most exciting modern cities in the world.

The Common Market Country

The Kingdom of the Netherlands was one of the original six members of the European Economic Community—the Common Market. This is not surprising, for with their long history as a trading nation the Dutch were aware of the great benefits that would come from having a wider market for their products.

Although agriculture remains the economic mainstay of the country, the Dutch have been quick to benefit from the new industrial revolution based on oil, gas, chemicals and electronics. Almost forty per cent of the working population are employed in industry.

The "Euromast" in Rotterdam—a symbol of the Netherlands. Visitors have a wonderful panoramic view of the world's largest port from the observation windows at the top

One example of the prosperity of the Netherlands—its excellent and constantly expanding road system. This cloverleaf crossing is in Utrecht

The vast reserves of natural gas discovered at Groningen in 1962 helped to make Holland less dependent on oil—almost half the country's energy is now supplied by natural gas. Since entry in to the E.E.C., Rotterdam has expanded as an industrial port, handling more tonnage than any other port in the world.

As hardworking now as they have ever been, the Dutch have won back their position as one of Europe's most prosperous countries. This is due entirely to the Dutch worker's dedication to his job.

As a result, his country—as part of the Common Market—is, for its size, one of the richest countries in the world, with a standard of living unsurpassed by any other.

Index